Breathe the Wind,
Drink the Rain

Breathe the Wind, Drink the Rain

Notes on Being Alive

Douglas Wood

NORTH STAR PRESS OF ST. CLOUD, INC.
St. Cloud, Minnesota

Dedicated . . .

To those who have taken the path to themselves.
To those still looking for it.

Printed in the United States of America

Published by
North Star Press of St. Cloud, Inc.
St. Cloud, Minnesota

www.northstarpress.com

Dear Reader,

This is a little book of advice. Advice on what? I thought you might ask that. Well, it began as an answer to a question I've often received on book tours: "How do you get to be a writer?" But as the piece developed, I found it had very little— all right, nothing—to do with being a writer, exactly, and a whole lot to do with being a Person. When the time came to title it, however, *How to Be a Person* seemed a bit of a far reach.

So, I leave it up to you. If you like the title I finally chose (as I rather do), leave it. If you can think of a better one, you have my permission to cross this one out and write yours on the cover. In any case, if this small volume helps you or someone you love to smile, or think, or get through a rough patch, or see sunrises or smell honeysuckle, or even become a writer (or carpenter or short-order cook), then I shall be happy indeed.

DW

P.S. Please buy the book before you change the title.

Wake Up.

Notice how things grow.

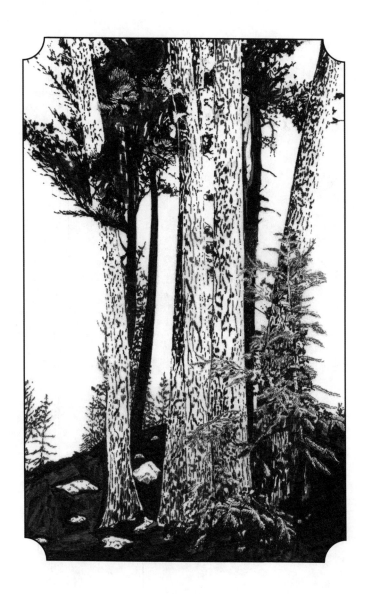

Don't be afraid to
    see what you see,
  hear what you hear,
      think what you think,
  or feel what you feel.

Attend sunrises.

Watch turtles.

Spend time with what you love.

Waste time with whom you love.

Save time with . . .
Forget about saving time.

Have a favorite chair.

Keep your windows clean.

Make a great "To Do" list.
Do most of it.

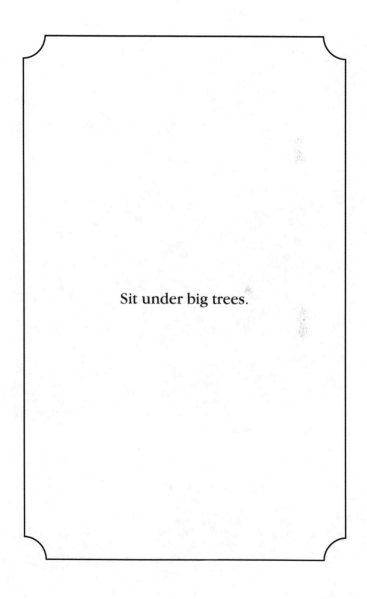

Sit under big trees.

Skinny dip.

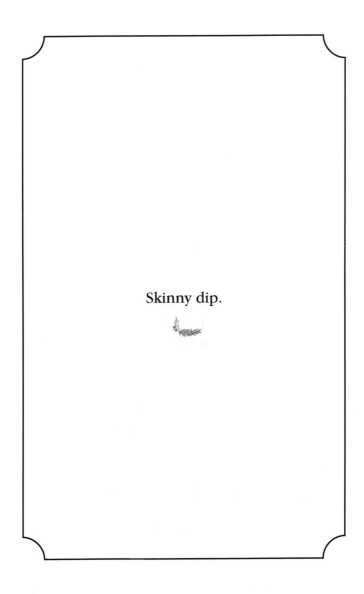

Learn to brew good coffee,
even if you don't drink it.

Smell honeysuckle.

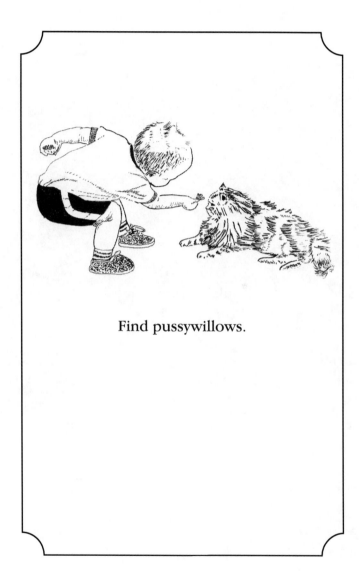

Find pussywillows.

Be smart.
Think of dumb things
And do the opposite.

Pack light.

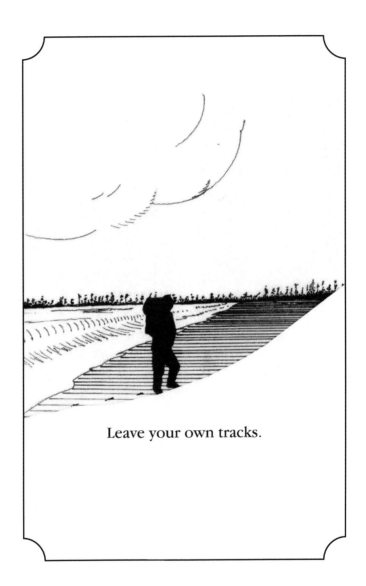

Leave your own tracks.

Travel well,
but
Be Where You Are Now.

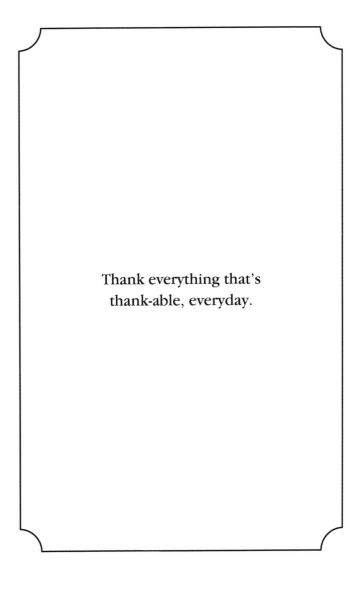

Thank everything that's
thank-able, everyday.

Look often at the moon and stars.

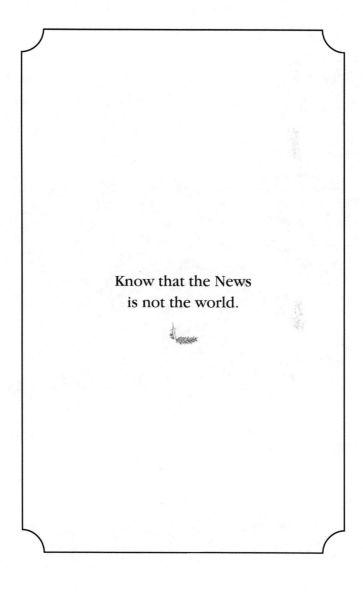

Know that the News
is not the world.

Accomplish things the way an
apple tree accomplishes apples.

Taste what you eat
and smell what you breathe.

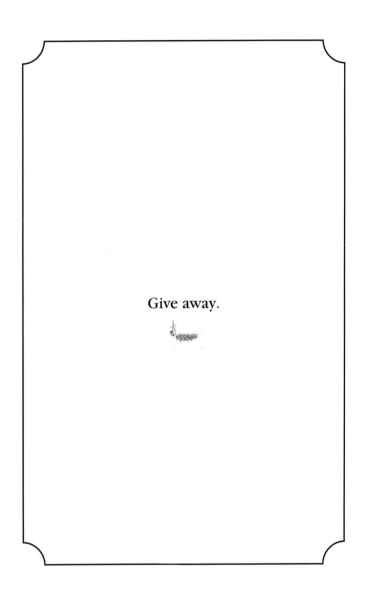

Give away.

Don't chase butterflies.

Be still; they'll land on you.

Tend your garden.

But learn to stop stepping on rakes.

Dream.

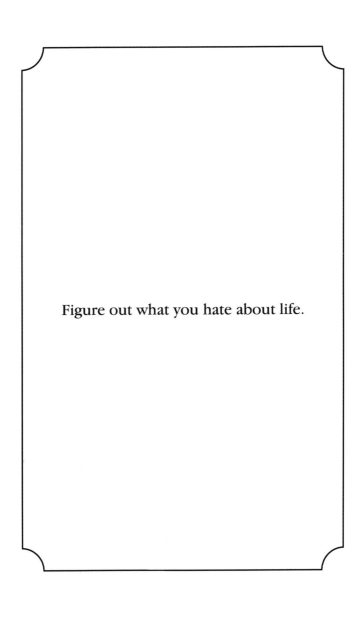

Figure out what you hate about life.

Figure out how to love life anyway.

Notice how *unusual* everything is.

Make friends with mystery.

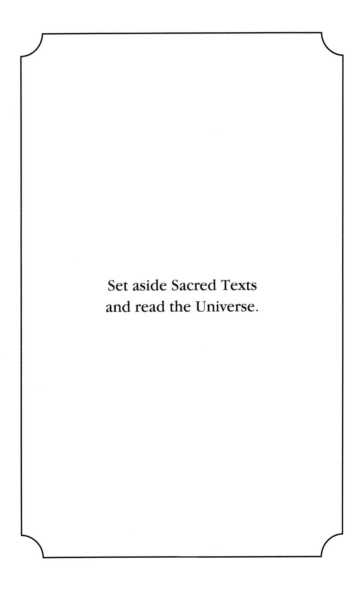

Set aside Sacred Texts
and read the Universe.

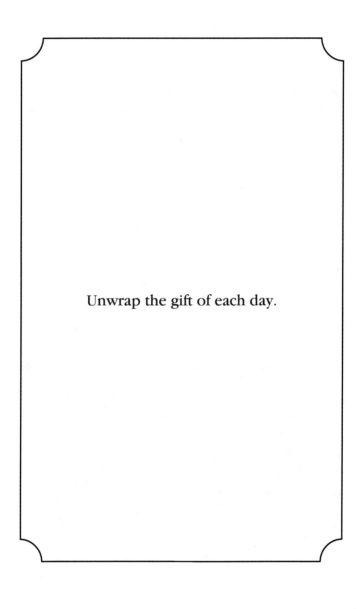

Unwrap the gift of each day.

Do the thing you fear.

Keep your pilot light lit.

Burn old wood,
    drink old wine,
trust old friends,
    and read old books.

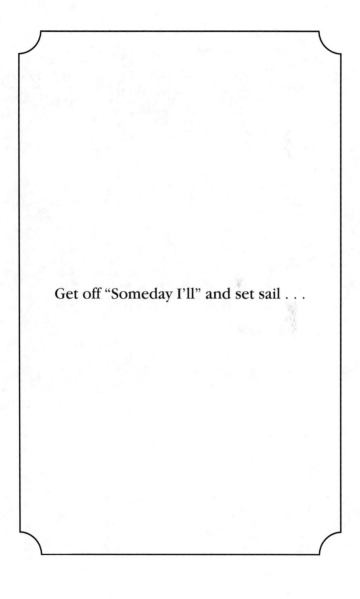

Get off "Someday I'll" and set sail . . .

For a *real* island . . .
For a point on the map . . .

For a point in your heart.

Remember . . . .
There is only one real question.

And the answer is Yes.